THE MULTIMILLIONAIRE METHOD

A STEP-BY-STEP SYSTEM FOR BUILDING WEALTH IN ANY BUSINESS

DESHAWN PRICE

HERITAGE
PUBLISHING

This book is dedicated to the builders — the ones who refused to stay where they started.
To those who got tired of potential without progress and chose discipline over delay.
To the early risers, late finishers, and quiet executors who kept moving when results were slow and doubt was loud.
To every operator who kept showing up when motivation disappeared and structure had to carry the load.
To the risk-takers who made decisions with imperfect information and learned forward instead of waiting forever.
To the men and women who chose ownership over excuses and systems over scattered effort.
This is for the overlooked, the underestimated, and the self-rebuilding.
For those who turned setbacks into strategy and pressure into process.
For the ones who decided that average was too small for their calling and consistency would be their advantage.
It is dedicated to disciplined action over flashy intention.
To repeatable habits over rare bursts.
To focus over noise, execution over emotion, and value over vanity.
And above all, it is dedicated to you — the reader who didn't just want inspiration, but implementation.

May you build what lasts, scale what works, and finish what you start.

"Results are not created by what you intend, admire, or announce — they are created by what you execute, repeat, and refine. Ideas spark the fire, but disciplined systems keep it burning. Decide boldly. Build deliberately. Operate relentlessly. Wealth follows the worker who shows up on schedule — not the dreamer who shows up when inspired."

FOREWORD

There are two kinds of business books in the world. The first kind inspires you while you read and leaves you unchanged when you stop. The second kind rearranges how you think, how you decide, and how you operate. *The Multimillionaire Method* belongs firmly in the second category.

What you are about to read is not a celebration of talent, luck, or perfect timing. It is a blueprint for execution. It does not promise shortcuts. It does not flatter hesitation. It does not suggest that success is reserved for a gifted few. Instead, it puts the spotlight where real wealth is actually built — on disciplined decisions, repeatable systems, operational focus, and personal ownership.

That may sound simple, but do not confuse simple with easy. Simple scales. Simple repeats. Simple survives pressure. Complexity often hides weakness, but structured simplicity produces strength. This book brings you back to the fundamentals that actually move financial outcomes: decisive action, measurable production, scalable processes, and disciplined follow-through.

You will notice quickly that the voice of this work is

direct. That is intentional. Wealth building is not improved by vagueness. Clarity creates movement. Throughout these pages, you will be challenged to confront comfortable excuses, costly distractions, and unproductive patterns. Not to condemn you — but to free you. The fastest path forward is honest diagnosis followed by structured action.

What makes this method powerful is that it is transferable. It is not tied to one industry, one platform, or one personality type. Whether you are building a company, a practice, a product line, a service operation, or a personal brand, the principles here apply because they are operational, not ornamental. They are built around how value is created, delivered, measured, and multiplied.

You will also find that this book refuses to romanticize motivation. Inspiration is welcomed — but not trusted as a primary fuel source. Systems, standards, and habits carry the load here. That is not cold — it is dependable. When emotion fluctuates, structure sustains. When conditions change, process adapts. When pressure rises, discipline pays.

As you read, do not treat these chapters as information to collect. Treat them as instructions to implement. Mark the parts that require a decision. Schedule the parts that require action. Build the parts that require structure. The return on this book will not come from agreement — it will come from application.

You are not being invited merely to think differently. You are being invited to operate differently.

If you accept that invitation — fully, practically, immediately — the results will not be theoretical. They will be measurable. They will be repeatable. And over time, they will be transformative.

Turn the page ready to build.

PREFACE

This book was not written for spectators. It was written for operators.

It was written for the builder who is tired of circling success instead of constructing it. For the entrepreneur who has notebooks full of ideas but wants systems full of results. For the leader who no longer wants inspiration alone, but implementation that compounds. If you are looking for comfort reading, this will stretch you. If you are looking for practical transformation, this will serve you.

The central claim of this book is simple and unapologetic: wealth is not mysterious, but it is methodical. Across industries, markets, and personalities, the same operational truths keep appearing. Decisive action beats prolonged hesitation. Systems beat scattered effort. Discipline beats emotional bursts. Focus beats frenzy. Ownership beats excuses. These are not slogans here — they are structural pillars.

You will notice the tone is direct, sometimes confrontational, often urgent. That is by design. Drift is expensive. Delay compounds quietly. Avoidance hides behind complexity. Polite language rarely interrupts unproductive patterns, but clear language can. This book speaks plainly because results respond to clarity. You deserve instruction you can execute, not just ideas you can admire.

This is not a theory-heavy manual or a motivational pep talk. It is a field guide for operational wealth building. Each section is built to move you from concept to calendar, from insight to action, from intention to measurable behavior. You will be repeatedly called to decide, to schedule, to build, to track, and to refine. Reading without doing will produce very little. Reading and executing will produce change.

You do not need perfect conditions to use this method. You do not need elite credentials, rare talent, or ideal timing. You need willingness to operate with structure and persist with discipline. The method works wherever value can be created and delivered — which means it works where you are, if you are willing to apply it.

As you move through these pages, pause often enough to implement. Turn chapters into checklists. Turn principles into procedures. Turn challenges into commitments. The speed of your execution will matter more than the speed of your reading.

This preface is your starting line, not your finish line.

Build accordingly.

INTRODUCTION

Most people say they want wealth. Almost nobody wants the process that creates it. That is the uncomfortable truth this book refuses to soften.

The Multimillionaire Method is not built for dreamers, dabblers, or chronic "researchers." It is built for operators — people willing to trade excuses for execution and comfort for compounding results. If you are looking for inspirational stories without operational structure, close this book now. Wealth does not come from hype. It comes from repeatable, measurable action applied with discipline over time.

The marketplace does not pay intention. It pays value delivered at scale. It does not reward potential. It rewards production. Many talented people remain financially stuck because they confuse knowledge with movement and planning with progress. This method draws a hard line between activity and advancement. Motion is not momentum. Effort is not equity. Busy is not profitable.

You will be told that success requires luck, connections, or perfect timing. It does not. It requires leverage, systems, positioning, and the courage to make decisions before you feel ready. The truth is polarizing: most financial struggle is not caused by lack of opportunity — it is caused by lack of structured execution. The good news is that execution can be learned, installed, and repeated.

This book presents a step-by-step operating system for building wealth in any business model — service, product, digital, local, or global. The principles are model-agnostic and results-driven. You will learn how to think in assets, engineer income streams, design scalable processes, and measure what actually matters.

No fluff. No motivational padding. No fantasy shortcuts.

You will either build systems — or you will work inside someone else's.

The method is here. The decision is yours.

1

EXECUTION BEATS INTELLIGENCE — WHY SMART PEOPLE STAY BROKE

Execution beats intelligence in the real world of wealth creation, and that statement will bother people who built their identity on being the smartest person in the room. The marketplace does not award trophies for potential, only payment for production. You can be brilliant and broke at the same time if your brilliance never leaves the notebook. Ideas do not deposit checks — implemented systems do. Knowledge is only power when it is converted into scheduled behavior. Smart people often become trapped in analysis loops while disciplined executors quietly build income streams. Intelligence asks, "What is the optimal path?" while execution asks, "What is the next step?" Wealth answers the second question, not the first. If you want multimillionaire results, you must become addicted to finishing, not just thinking. From this moment forward, measure your days by completed outputs, not clever insights.

Let me give you a picture you won't forget: a locked warehouse full of gold is still useless to the hungry owner without a key. Your intelligence is the warehouse, but execution is the key in your hand. I once watched two entrepreneurs start with equal knowledge and equal opportunity, yet five years later one owned assets and the other owned excuses. The difference was not education — it was daily action taken when motivation was low. One launched imperfect offers and improved them in public. The other redesigned logos, retitled plans, and waited for ideal timing. Perfection delayed one while progress paid the other. You don't get paid for preparing forever — you get paid for entering the arena. The multimillionaire method is not secret — it is scheduled. Do the revenue-producing task first each day before anything comfortable. Swing the hammer before you sharpen it again.

Overthinking is not a strategy — it is often fear with a spreadsheet. It feels responsible, sounds wise, and looks professional, but it quietly postpones your breakthrough. You tell yourself you are being careful when you are actually being cautious beyond usefulness. You claim you are refining when you are really avoiding exposure. But clarity is born from contact with reality, not isolation from it. The first version teaches more than the fifteenth draft. The first sales call teaches more than ten sales books. The first launch teaches more than a year of private planning. Action is the microscope of truth. If you want sharper vision, move closer through execution. Replace "What if it fails?" with "What will it teach?" Then move.

Here is a hard truth delivered with respect: information addiction is one of the most expensive habits smart people have. Courses feel productive, notes feel productive, highlighting feels productive — but none of them create cash flow by themselves. You can consume motivation daily and still produce nothing weekly. The wealthy convert learning into deadlines and deadlines into deliverables. They shorten the distance between instruction and implementation. They don't just ask, "What did I learn?" — they ask, "What did I deploy?" Every page should become a plan, every plan a task list, every task list a calendar block. Your calendar is your real business partner. If execution is not scheduled, it is imaginary. Put the work where the clock can see it.

Now breathe this in because it should lift your head — you are not incapable, you are under-executed. That is not an insult; that is an invitation. Under-execution can be corrected starting today with zero new talent. You don't need a new personality to become wealthy — you need a new pattern of behavior. Confidence is built by kept commitments to yourself. When you finish what you schedule, self-trust grows. When self-trust grows, risk tolerance rises. When risk tolerance rises, opportunity expands. This is not hype — it is psychological compounding. Start with small daily completions and guard them fiercely. Stack wins like bricks and watch identity change shape. You become what you repeatedly complete.

Let me ground this with a street-level illustration you can feel. A food truck owner who opens every day will out-earn a gourmet chef who never opens the doors. Consistency beats sophistication when sophistication never ships. The market rewards availability and reliability before it rewards elegance. Show up with the offer. Show up with the service. Show up with the follow-up. Your first version can be simple and still be profitable. Complexity is not a prerequisite for income — delivery is. Make it real, make it usable, make it available. Improve it after it is alive. Dead perfect ideas earn nothing.

Responsibility is the turning key in the multimillionaire method, and most people try to copy tactics without accepting ownership. They want the upside without the weight. But ownership is where power lives. When you own the outcome, you control the adjustment. No blaming algorithms, markets, childhood, competitors, or timing. Blame removes leverage while ownership restores it. Say, "If it's to be, it's through my disciplined execution." That sentence is not pressure — it is permission. It gives you authority over your next move. Track your numbers, track your actions, track your follow-through. What gets measured gets multiplied. Face facts fast and fix forward.

Expect resistance when you begin executing at a higher level, because growth always irritates your comfort zone. Your mind will suggest delay dressed as logic. Your emotions will suggest rest dressed as wisdom. But discipline is doing the important work before the urgent noise. You don't wait to feel like it — you act to become it. Athletes train on schedule, not on mood. Builders build on timeline, not on emotion. Producers produce on target, not on preference. Install a non-negotiable daily output quota. Hit it whether you feel sharp or slow. Especially when you feel slow. That is how identity hardens into reliability. That is how wealth starts trusting you.

Let's talk about failure the right way, because fear of it keeps intelligent people frozen. Failure is data wearing work clothes. It is not a verdict on your worth — it is feedback on your method. Every failed campaign teaches targeting. Every rejected offer teaches positioning. Every low response teaches messaging. Treat results like instruments, not insults. Adjust variables, not vision. The only true business failure is quitting measurement and quitting movement. Stay in motion with awareness. Debrief, refine, relaunch. Speed of correction matters more than perfection of first attempt. Fall forward with notes in your hand.

Here is your step-by-step execution framework —

simple, repeatable, profitable. Pick one business model and stay with it long enough to learn its seasons. Define one core value offer that solves a real problem. Set a public launch date to create healthy pressure. Schedule daily revenue-producing actions before administrative work. Track outputs, not hours. Review results weekly and adjust precisely. Multiply what converts and eliminate what distracts. Build systems from repeated actions. Then scale with people and process. Execution is not one act — it is a lifestyle rhythm.

Lift your standard starting now, because the line between broke and multimillionaire is often behavioral, not intellectual. Decide that you are a finisher, not a dabbler. Decide that you ship, not stall. Decide that you measure, not guess. Decide that you act, not admire. Let others debate theories while you deploy offers. Let others wait for certainty while you build capability. Let others polish while you publish. The market does not need more thinkers — it needs more disciplined deliverers. Become one. Start today. Execute before the day ends.

2

STOP STUDYING SUCCESS — START SHIPPING RESULTS

Stop studying success like it is a museum exhibit and start shipping results like it is your profession. You don't build wealth by admiring winning strategies — you build it by deploying working ones. Too many intelligent people have shelves full of notes and bank accounts full of hesitation. Information feels safe because it carries no risk of rejection. Shipping results feels dangerous because it invites evaluation. But the marketplace only pays for what you release, not what you research. A recipe never fed a family until someone turned on the stove. Your breakthrough is not hiding in another lesson — it is hiding behind your first launch. Draw a line today between preparation and production. Decide that from this point forward you are a builder, not a browser.

Let me give you a street-level picture you can't dodge. Imagine a warehouse packed with perfectly designed products that never leave the loading dock. Beautiful packaging, brilliant engineering, flawless labeling — and zero revenue. That is what unlaunched potential looks like. I once met a founder who redesigned his offer for eighteen months and another who launched in eighteen days. The fast launcher earned feedback, customers, and momentum. The slow perfectionist earned opinions, revisions, and delay. Which one learned faster, grew faster, and earned faster. Motion creates instruction that theory never reveals. Your job is not to look ready — your job is to be in motion. Ship version one this week, not version perfect next year.

Here is the uncomfortable truth that sets executors free: studying can become a sophisticated hiding place. You say you're "getting clarity" when you're really avoiding exposure. You say you're "building a foundation" when you're really postponing judgment. But clarity comes from contact, not contemplation. A pilot learns most in the air, not only in the classroom. A seller learns most in conversations, not only in courses. A builder learns most with tools in hand, not diagrams on screen. Action is the furnace that burns fog into focus. If you want sharper direction, take a visible step. Replace private preparation with public progress. Do the work where results can answer you.

Let me encourage you while I challenge you — you are not behind in knowledge, you are behind in release. That means your gap is closable starting now. You don't need another certification to start serving people. You need a calendar, a commitment, and a shipped offer. Start small, start simple, start visible. One posted product, one live service, one published page, one open door. Small launches beat large delays every time. Confidence grows from completed cycles, not completed courses. Stack shipped work like bricks and watch self-belief rise. You are more ready than your fear admits. Prove it with output.

Wealth does not reward the most informed — it rewards the most consistent producers. That line should wake you up and calm you down at the same time. You don't have to know everything — you have to do the next thing. A farmer does not study soil forever — he plants on schedule. A musician does not practice silently forever — she performs publicly. A business builder does not plan privately forever — they sell visibly. Production is proof of seriousness. Output is evidence of ownership. Shipping is how intention becomes income. Set a daily production quota and hit it before noon. Let learning support your work, not replace it.

Let's talk about your excuses with respect and resolve. "I need more time" usually means "I haven't set a deadline." "I need more clarity" usually means "I haven't tested the market." "I'm not ready" usually means "I'm afraid to be seen trying." These are not character flaws — they are correctable patterns. Replace vague goals with scheduled deliverables. Replace private standards with public deadlines. Replace emotional hesitation with mechanical action. You don't negotiate with the alarm clock — you respond to it. Treat your production window like an appointment with your future wealth. Non-negotiable means non-negotiable. Execute anyway.

Here's a simple story you'll remember. Two authors started the same year with the same dream. One studied publishing trends, cover psychology, and platform strategy for three years. The other wrote, published, learned, and published again. Guess which one built readership, revenue, and reach. Imperfect books in readers' hands beat perfect manuscripts in drawers. The market trains you faster than mentors alone. Feedback is fuel when you use it instead of fearing it. Publish, measure, improve, repeat. That loop is the multimillionaire method in motion. Shorten the distance between attempt and adjustment. Speed of iteration beats depth of hesitation.

You must reframe failure starting today or you will keep

postponing profit. Failure is not a stop sign — it is a steering signal. When a shipment underperforms, you adjust the message, not your mission. When an offer flops, you refine the audience, not your ambition. Every shipped result teaches you something measurable. Every unshipped idea teaches you nothing practical. Data is born from doing. Treat results like instruments on a dashboard. Read them, respond to them, relaunch with intelligence earned in motion. Falling forward pays better than standing still. Stay in the arena long enough to get smarter through contact.

Discipline is the bridge between intention and income, and you build it with daily boards, not dramatic speeches. Install a shipping ritual that happens whether you feel inspired or not. Professionals produce on schedule, amateurs produce on emotion. You are building a professional wealth identity now. That means you track outputs, not moods. You finish tasks, not just start them. You close loops, not just open tabs. Execution is a muscle — train it daily. Completion is a habit — practice it hourly. Become known to yourself as someone who delivers. Identity follows evidence.

Let's make this practical so you can move today, not someday. Choose one value offer that solves one painful problem. Set a launch date within seven days, not seven months. Create the simplest usable version and release it. Tell real people directly and invite response. Track every reaction and refine fast. Improve the message, tighten the promise, clarify the result. Ship again with upgrades, not apologies. Repeat until traction appears. Momentum is built through cycles, not contemplation. Start the first cycle now.

You are not called to admire multimillionaire methods — you are called to apply them. Execution is your unfair advantage if you embrace it relentlessly. Let others collect quotes while you collect customers. Let others watch trends while you test offers. Let others wait for perfect while you release profitable. Decide that shipping is your new identity. Say it out loud and schedule it in ink. Move before doubt votes again. Produce before comfort negotiates again. Stop studying success and start shipping results today.

3

YOUR INCOME IS NOT LIMITED — YOUR STANDARDS ARE

Your income is not limited — your standards are, and that truth will either offend your excuses or unlock your future. Money rarely rises above the level of behavior you are willing to repeat consistently. You say you want more income, but your calendar says you want more comfort. You say you want expansion, but your habits say you want ease. Wealth is not blocked by fate — it is filtered by standards. Show me your daily non-negotiables and I will show you your financial trajectory. The marketplace pays people who keep higher promises to their schedule than to their moods. This is not condemnation — this is leverage in your hands. Raise what you require from yourself and you raise what returns to you. Starting today, your standards become your strategy.

Let me make this plain with a picture you can feel. A thermostat does not argue with the weather — it sets the temperature and the system responds. Your standards are your internal thermostat for income and impact. If you set them low, performance cools down to match. If you set them high, behavior heats up to reach them. I once worked with two operators in the same field with the same tools and the same hours. One had a minimum daily output standard and the other had a "try my best" intention. The one with the standard doubled results in months. The one with intentions doubled explanations. Set a number, set a quota, set a floor. Then refuse to negotiate with yourself about hitting it.

Here is the truth most people dodge: you don't get what you desire — you get what you tolerate. You tolerate distraction, so you get delay. You tolerate inconsistency, so you get instability. You tolerate average effort, so you get average income. That is not cruelty — that is cause and effect wearing work boots. Raise your tolerance for disciplined effort and lower your tolerance for wasted time. Stop excusing the patterns that are pricing your life too low. You are not stuck — you are under-standardized. Standards are decisions pre-made so emotions don't get a vote later. Write yours down and live by them loudly.

Let me encourage you right in the middle of this push — you are capable of higher standards than you've been practicing. You don't need a personality transplant to level up your life. You need a rule upgrade and a routine upgrade. Think of standards like guardrails on a mountain road — they don't restrict freedom, they protect progress. When your work start time is fixed, your output stabilizes. When your production target is fixed, your focus sharpens. When your follow-up rule is fixed, your pipeline grows. Structure is not a prison — it is a profit partner. Install it. Trust it. Run inside it.

Consider the athlete who trains whether the crowd shows up or not. The standard is the workout, not the applause. The wealthy think the same way about value creation. They produce whether motivation is loud or quiet. They prospect when it's inconvenient. They refine when it's boring. They execute when it's repetitive. That is why they get paid when others get ready. Repetition is not your enemy — it is your income engine. Fall in love with the reps that produce results. Schedule them daily and protect them fiercely.

Let's get polarizing for your benefit, not your shame. Some people say they want seven-figure income with five-figure discipline. That math never balances. High income is rented daily through high standards of behavior. You cannot out-dream low execution. You cannot out-affirm weak structure. You cannot out-visualize poor follow-through. The bridge between desire and dollars is disciplined delivery. Raise your floor, not just your ceiling. Make your worst day of execution better than your old best day. That is how identity upgrades stick.

Here's a simple story that carries weight. A shop owner cleaned his store to inspection level every night, even when sales were slow. A competitor cleaned only when customers complained. Months later, one had loyal repeat buyers and the other had discount hunters only. The difference was not location — it was standard. Excellence attracts trust before it attracts scale. People feel your standards before they analyze your pricing. Tighten your process and watch confidence rise around you. Improve what you control immediately. Excellence is a magnet when it becomes normal.

Now bring this down to daily action so it pays you, not just inspires you. Set three non-negotiable daily standards tied to revenue and value. One creation standard, one connection standard, one completion standard. Define them in numbers, not feelings. Track them in ink, not intention. Review them at day's end without excuses. If you miss, adjust tomorrow — but never erase the standard. Standards are anchors, not suggestions. Live by them and let results catch up.

You must also raise your recovery standard, because resilience is part of wealth. When you fall short, your standard is not perfection — it is fast correction. No spirals, no self-pity marathons, no quitting weeks. Reset quickly and re-enter the work. Champions are not those who never slip — they are those who re-grip fast. Build a bounce-back rule into your life. Failure gets one day, adjustment gets the next. Keep moving. Keep measuring. Keep improving.

Let me speak to your identity now, because standards stick best when they become personal. You are not someone trying harder — you are someone who operates higher. You are not hoping for better — you are requiring better from yourself. Say it until it feels natural and then prove it with behavior. Identity is built through repeated evidence. Each kept standard is a vote for your future self. Cast those votes daily and loudly. Become known — first to yourself — as reliable under pressure. That reputation will pay you.

Your income is not capped by the economy, your past, or your personality. It is shaped by the standards you enforce when no one is watching. Raise them and your strategy improves automatically. Raise them and your schedule tightens automatically. Raise them and your output climbs naturally. This is not magic — it is mechanics. Decide your new standards today and install them this week. Put them on your wall and in your calendar. Live them without negotiation. Your next income level is on the other side of your next standard upgrade. Step across now.

4

BUSY IS A LIE — ONLY PRODUCTION PAYS

Busy is a lie that comforts you while your potential starves, and only production pays in the economy that actually matters. Activity is not achievement, motion is not progress, and noise is not income. You can answer emails all day and still avoid the one call that creates revenue. You can attend meetings all week and still dodge the one decision that creates momentum. Busy feels productive because it is loud, visible, and socially acceptable. Production feels risky because it is measurable, exposed, and accountable. But the scoreboard of wealth only counts finished value delivered to real people. A spinning wheel makes motion but goes nowhere. Today you stop spinning and start producing.

Picture two workers on the same construction site for a moment and lock this image in your mind. One carries tools back and forth, rearranges supplies, checks lists, and looks constantly in motion. The other lays bricks in straight lines hour after hour. At the end of the day one is tired and one has a wall. Effort is not the same as output, and the market pays for walls, not sweat. I once coached a founder who worked twelve-hour days and shipped nothing for months. We cut his task list in half and doubled his deliverables in two weeks. He wasn't lazy — he was scattered. Focus turned motion into money. Choose the bricks, not the busyness.

Here is the truth most people resist because it removes their favorite hiding place. Busyness is often procrastination with better branding. It lets you feel responsible while avoiding the hard, high-value moves. You organize instead of offering. You plan instead of pitching. You polish instead of publishing. But avoidance dressed as effort is still avoidance. If a task does not create, sell, improve, or deliver value, it is support work at best. Support work must never replace production work. Each day must contain visible value creation. Schedule production first and let busy tasks fill leftover space only.

Let me steady you while I stretch you, because you are not failing — you are misallocating energy. That is fixable starting today with a pen and a clock. You don't need more hours — you need protected production windows. Think of your day like a farm and your hours like fields. If you plant nothing, you harvest nothing, no matter how busy you walked the fence. Production is planting — visible, countable, repeatable value creation. Protect two daily planting blocks with zero distraction. Phone down, tabs closed, targets clear. When the block starts, you produce or you sit — nothing else. Train your nervous system to associate that time with output only.

Consider the restaurant kitchen at dinner rush and learn from the heat. The chef is not busy — the chef is producing plates. Orders come in and finished meals go out. No one gets paid for chopping forever without serving. The wealthy run their business day like a kitchen, not a classroom. Tickets in, value out, repeat again. They measure throughput, not motion. They track finished units, not attempted tasks. You must think in completed deliverables, not consumed hours. Ask daily, what did I ship, not how long did I try. Then raise that number tomorrow.

Let's get bold and a little uncomfortable because comfort has been overpaid in your schedule. Some people brag about being busy the way others brag about being productive. That is like bragging about being at the gym without lifting weight. Presence is not performance. Time spent is not value sent. Your calendar can be full and your pipeline empty at the same time. Stop worshiping full days and start demanding finished outputs. Replace to-do lists with done lists that matter. If it doesn't move revenue, reach, or results, it doesn't lead the day. Lead with production or drift with busyness.

Here is a simple story that draws a sharp line. A creator posted one useful piece of content daily while another spent months designing a perfect brand kit. The daily poster built audience, feedback, and sales. The brand perfectionist built folders, drafts, and delay. One chose visible production and grew in public. The other chose private preparation and stayed invisible. Imperfect value delivered beats perfect value delayed. The market forgives rough edges but ignores silence. Ship useful before beautiful. Improve after impact. Publish before polish becomes a prison.

Now let's turn this into a working system you can apply before this day ends. Define your top three production activities tied directly to income or measurable value. Put them at the top of your day before messages, meetings, and maintenance. Assign a numeric output target to each one. Track completion visibly where you cannot ignore it. When distractions appear, label them support tasks and park them. Finish production first, then support second. Build a scoreboard for yourself and update it daily. What gets seen gets improved. What gets measured gets multiplied.

You also need a recovery rule for the days that slip, because resilience keeps production alive long term. When you miss a production block, you don't spiral — you reschedule within twenty-four hours. No guilt marathons, only adjustment moves. Professionals reset fast and return to output. Your identity is not "busy person" — it is "reliable producer." Say it and back it with behavior. Identity grows where repetition goes. Stack production days like coins and watch confidence compound. Miss small, correct fast, continue strong. That is how momentum survives real life.

Let me speak directly to the part of you that knows you were built for more than motion. You are not here to be exhausted — you are here to be effective. You are not called to look active — you are called to create value. Busy is a smoke screen, but production is a spotlight. Step into the spotlight with finished work. Deliver something real, measurable, useful today. Send the proposal, launch the offer, publish the asset, make the ask. Let results start talking back to you. Only production pays, and you are now a producer. Start before this hour ends.

5

THE COMFORT TRAP — WHY STABILITY IS THE ENEMY OF WEALTH

Comfort is not harmless — it is expensive, and in the world of wealth building it is often the silent enemy wearing soft clothes. Stability feels safe, predictable, respectable, and responsible, but it can quietly freeze your growth in place. You were not built to merely maintain — you were built to multiply. The moment your main goal becomes comfort instead of creation, your expansion begins to shrink. Wealth is rarely born in padded rooms and predictable patterns. It is forged where uncertainty meets disciplined action. You don't drift into multimillionaire territory — you climb into it with intention and friction. If your days feel too safe, your results will stay too small. This is not an attack on peace — it is a warning about stagnation. Choose constructive discomfort on purpose starting now.

Let me give you a picture that will stick in your mind longer than a slogan. A muscle wrapped in padding never grows stronger — it grows weaker. An arm in a cast becomes smaller, not safer. I once worked with a talented operator who kept the same modest offer for years because it "worked well enough." It paid the bills but buried the upside. When he finally stretched, upgraded, and risked rejection, his revenue tripled in a year. His danger was not failure — it was familiarity. Comfort had him parked below his capacity. You must audit your routines for hidden casts. If it never stretches you, it never strengthens you.

Here is the truth most people avoid because it confronts their favorite excuse. Stability can become a sophisticated stall tactic. You call it being responsible when it is actually being fearful. You call it being patient when it is actually being passive. But patience works only when paired with purposeful motion. A parked car does not arrive early — it arrives nowhere. Progress requires pressure applied in a direction. You don't need reckless risk, but you do need repeated reach. Schedule one uncomfortable growth action daily. Make stretch your standard.

Let me steady your heart while I stretch your thinking, because this message is for your elevation, not your shame. You are not wrong for wanting security — you are wrong for worshiping it. Security is a tool, not a throne. The strongest builders create safety nets while still climbing higher. They build reserves and take calculated shots. They test new offers while serving current clients. They expand skill while income is steady. That is wise aggression, not careless gambling. You can be grounded and growing at the same time. Install a growth lane beside your stability lane.

Think about the pilot who keeps the plane on the runway because the runway feels stable. The runway is safe, flat, and familiar — and completely useless for travel if you never leave it. Lift requires resistance and motion. Altitude requires throttle and commitment. Your runway is your current comfort zone. Your throttle is decisive action beyond it. You cannot soar and stay parked. Increase thrust in one key area this month. Launch something that stretches your capability.

Let's get polarizing in a way that wakes you up instead of wears you down. Many people say they want wealth, but what they really want is comfortable predictability. Those two desires often collide. Wealth demands experimentation, iteration, exposure, and adaptation. Comfort demands repetition, insulation, and control. One grows capacity while the other protects routine. You must choose which master leads your calendar. If every week looks the same, your income will too. Predictable effort produces predictable earnings. Insert controlled disruption into your schedule.

Here is a simple story with sharp edges and useful truth. Two employees received the same steady paycheck for years. One used nights to build a side system and learn high-value skills. The other used nights to protect comfort and recover routine. Five years later one owned assets and options. The other owned stability and surprise bills. The difference was not intelligence — it was stretch behavior. Evenings became expansion time for one and escape time for the other. Small discomforts compound into large advantages. Reclaim your off-hours for upward movement.

Now let's translate this into a step-by-step wealth behavior you can execute immediately. Identify one area where you have been coasting instead of climbing. Define a measurable stretch target attached to that area. Put a deadline on it that makes you slightly nervous. Break it into weekly discomfort actions. Track completion publicly or with an accountability partner. Reward execution, not ease. Review progress every seven days without emotional editing. Adjust tactics but keep the stretch goal. Growth lives on the other side of repeated reach.

You must also build a resilience rule because discomfort

will talk back. When stretch creates friction, your mind will suggest retreat. Expect that voice and plan your answer now. Your answer is scheduled action anyway. Courage is not loud — it is consistent. It shows up again after doubt speaks. It executes again after fatigue votes. It advances again after fear whispers. Install a no-retreat-once-started rule for key growth projects. Finish the climb you begin.

Let me speak directly to your identity because wealth-level behavior sticks when it becomes personal. You are not a comfort seeker — you are a capacity builder. You are not here to be merely stable — you are here to be scalable. Say that until it sounds like you. Back it with stretch decisions weekly. Identity is reinforced by repeated brave acts. Each discomfort completed is a vote for your future self. Cast those votes aggressively and consistently. Become known to yourself as someone who leans into growth.

Stability is not evil, but it is dangerous when it becomes your ceiling instead of your floor. Use it as a platform, not a prison. Stand on it and build higher. Fund your stretch from your base. Expand while anchored, not instead of anchored. This is disciplined ambition, not reckless motion. The multimillionaire method requires constructive discomfort applied consistently. Choose one stretch move today and schedule it in ink. Move before comfort negotiates you back to average. Your next wealth level is waiting outside the comfort trap. Step out now.

6

IDEAS DON'T MAKE MILLIONS — SYSTEMS DO

Ideas don't make millions — systems do, and that truth cuts straight through the fantasy that one brilliant thought will change your financial life. Inspiration is common, but infrastructure is rare. Everyone has ideas in the shower, on the drive, at the conference, after the podcast. Very few build repeatable machines that turn value into revenue on schedule. An idea is a spark, but a system is an engine. Sparks are exciting for a moment, engines move weight for miles. You don't need a better idea right now — you need a better operating structure. Wealth is not built on flashes — it is built on flows. Decide today that you will become a system builder, not an idea collector. Write that decision where you can see it and act on it before the day ends.

Let me give you a picture you can't shake loose. A single bucket of water feels helpful, but a pipeline changes cities. I once met a creator with dozens of clever product concepts and almost no sales. Another had one simple offer connected to a repeatable follow-up and referral system. Guess who had predictable income and growing opportunity. The idea generator was busy and broke. The system builder was focused and flourishing. Buckets require constant lifting, pipelines require upfront building. Stop carrying buckets when you could be laying pipe. Start designing flow instead of chasing bursts.

Here is the uncomfortable truth that frees disciplined builders. New ideas are often a socially acceptable form of procrastination. You tell yourself you're being innovative when you're actually being inconsistent. You jump to the next concept before the current one gets structure. But unfinished ideas don't fail — they evaporate. The market never even gets a vote. A tested system beats an untested breakthrough every time. Depth pays more than novelty. Stay with one value path long enough to systemize it. Refuse idea-hopping and commit to idea-building.

Let me encourage you while I press you forward, because you are not short on creativity — you are short on containers. Your mind produces sparks, but your calendar needs processes. Think of a system as a container that holds your effort steady. When effort is steady, results become predictable. When results are predictable, scale becomes possible. You don't rise by intensity alone — you rise by repeatability. Install repeatable steps for lead generation, value delivery, and follow-up. Make your business boring in process and exciting in results. Stability of method creates scalability of outcome. Build the container now.

Think about the difference between a recipe and a restaurant chain. A recipe can be brilliant and still feed only a few people. A chain has training, timing, sourcing, quality checks, and duplication rules. That is a system at work. The multimillionaire method thinks in replication, not inspiration. Can your value be delivered the same way twice without you reinventing it. Can someone else follow your steps and get similar results. If not, you have talent — but not yet a system. Document what works while you work it. Turn success into steps.

Let's get bold enough to break a dangerous myth. Lone genius is overrated in wealth building. Reliable systems with average people outperform brilliant chaos with exceptional people. You don't scale personalities — you scale processes. Your goal is not to be heroic — it is to be repeatable. Heroes burn out, systems endure. Build checklists, scripts, templates, automations, and routines. Reduce guesswork and increase consistency. Make excellence easier to repeat than mediocrity. That is how empires quietly form.

Here is a short story that draws a bright line. Two service providers had equal skill and equal demand. One handled each client from scratch every time. The other built onboarding steps, communication templates, and delivery workflows. One grew tired and capped income. The other grew structured and expanded capacity. Same talent, different trajectory. Structure multiplied one and exhausted the other. Your ceiling is often a system problem, not a skill problem. Solve the structure and lift the limit.

Now let's move this from insight to instruction so it pays you quickly. Choose your core offer and map the full value path step by step. From first contact to final delivery, write every repeatable action. Turn each action into a checklist item. Turn each checklist into a documented process. Improve the process after each cycle. Measure time, quality, and conversion at every stage. Remove friction and automate what repeats. Train yourself first, then train others. Build once, benefit repeatedly.

You must also systemize your improvement or growth will stall after early wins. Install a weekly review ritual that examines numbers and bottlenecks. No emotion, just evidence. What step slows flow. What step leaks leads. What step lowers quality. Fix the step, not the dream. Continuous refinement beats occasional overhaul. Small process upgrades compound into massive performance gains. Schedule your review like a board meeting with your future millions. Keep it sacred.

Let me talk to your identity now because system builders think differently about themselves. You are not just a worker — you are an architect of repeatable value. You are not chasing income — you are constructing flow. Say that until it feels natural. Then prove it with documentation and design. Each process you build is a brick in your wealth machine. Each checklist is a confidence multiplier. Each automation is a freedom lever. Build the machine and let it carry load. Stop pushing everything uphill alone.

Here is your next move, clear and immediate. Take one area of your work that feels heavy and redesign it into steps. Write them, order them, test them. Use them tomorrow exactly as written. Refine after execution, not before. Turn personal habit into documented process. Turn documented process into repeatable system. Turn repeatable system into scalable asset. This is how ideas become income engines. This is how effort becomes equity. Ideas don't make millions — systems do. Start building your first one today.

7

MOTIVATION IS WEAK — DISCIPLINE IS BANKABLE

Motivation is weak — discipline is bankable, and if that sentence stings a little, good, because it is trying to wake up your earning power. Motivation is emotional weather, discipline is structural steel. You cannot build a financial skyscraper on emotional forecasts. Some days you feel driven, some days you feel drained, and motivation disappears exactly when difficulty appears. But discipline shows up with or without applause. Discipline clocks in when feelings call out. Wealth is not built on emotional highs — it is built on scheduled standards. The multimillionaire method is not fueled by hype — it is fueled by habit. You don't need to feel ready — you need to be reliable. Decide now that reliability beats intensity every time.

Let me give you a picture you can carry into every workday. A power plant does not run on inspiration — it runs on systems and controls. No one walks in and says, "Let's generate electricity only when we feel excited." Output is scheduled, measured, and maintained. I once worked with a founder who chased motivation with podcasts and playlists but avoided structured work blocks. Revenue was inconsistent because behavior was inconsistent. When he installed fixed production hours, his results stabilized within weeks. Nothing magical happened — something mechanical did. He stopped waiting to feel like it and started acting like it. Structure replaced mood. Install your power plant schedule now.

Here is the truth most people dodge because it removes their favorite excuse. Waiting for motivation is a delay strategy, not a success strategy. It sounds wise but acts weak. You tell yourself timing matters when really discipline matters more. The farmer does not plant when inspired — he plants when it is time. The athlete does not train when emotional — she trains when scheduled. The builder does not pour concrete when motivated — he pours when prepared. Your income responds to consistency, not intensity. Replace emotional readiness with behavioral readiness. Put your key actions on the clock.

Let me encourage you right in the middle of this push, because discipline is not punishment — it is protection. It protects your goals from your moods. It protects your future from your impulses. It protects your progress from your distractions. Think of discipline like a bridge over emotional chaos. When feelings flood, discipline gives you a crossing. You don't need to be harder — you need to be steadier. Gentle consistency beats dramatic bursts. Build steady. Work steady. Deliver steady. That is bankable behavior.

Consider the difference between a savings account and loose cash on a table. Loose cash gets spent quickly and carelessly. A savings account grows because it is governed by rules. Discipline is the rule set that keeps your effort invested instead of wasted. Without rules, energy leaks. With rules, energy compounds. Set rules for start time, output targets, and completion standards. Follow them whether the day feels light or heavy. Rules remove debate and increase direction. Direction increases deposits. Make your work governed, not guessed.

Let's get bold enough to cut through a popular myth. Motivation-centered people start strong and stall often. Discipline-centered people start modest and scale steadily. One burns bright and fades. The other builds slow and lasts. Which one would you trust with a multimillion-dollar operation. Excitement is loud but short-lived. Discipline is quiet but long-lived. Stop chasing emotional fire and start building operational fuel. Install routines that run without drama. That is how professionals win.

Here is a short story that draws the contrast clearly. Two salespeople had equal talent and equal territory. One worked only when energized and inspired. The other worked a fixed call block daily no matter the mood. Guess who built the larger pipeline. Guess who had predictable commissions. The disciplined caller felt average but earned above average. The motivated caller felt great but earned inconsistently. Feelings lied — habits paid. Let habits lead your income. Fix your call block today.

Now let's make this practical so discipline becomes doable, not theoretical. Choose three daily non-negotiable actions tied directly to revenue or value creation. Assign them a fixed time window. Define a minimum completion number for each. Track them publicly or visually. Never miss twice in a row — that is your recovery rule. If you slip once, you correct immediately. Discipline is not perfection — it is rapid return. Build streaks and protect them fiercely. What you repeat grows roots.

You must also train your identity, because discipline sticks when it becomes personal. Stop saying you are trying to be consistent — say you are a consistent operator. Language shapes behavior more than you think. Identity drives repetition. Each kept commitment is a vote for that identity. Cast votes daily through action. When you keep your schedule, you strengthen your self-trust. Self-trust multiplies courage. Courage multiplies opportunity. Become dependable to yourself first.

Let me speak to the part of you that is tired of emotional roller coasters in progress and income. You are not broken because motivation fades — you are human. But you are powerful when discipline leads. You can build a life that runs on structure instead of spikes. You can create output that appears whether you feel brilliant or bland. That is freedom, not restriction. That is strength, not stiffness. That is bankable behavior in motion. Motivation is weak — discipline is bankable. Choose bankable starting today.

8

IF IT DOESN'T SCALE, IT DOESN'T STAY

If it doesn't scale, it doesn't stay, and that sentence should become a filter you run across every opportunity, offer, and obligation in your business life. Hard work alone is noble but not always profitable. Effort that cannot multiply will eventually exhaust you. You were not built to be the permanent engine — you were built to build the engine. Too many people create income that depends entirely on their constant presence. That is not a business — that is a job wearing your name tag. Wealth requires lift, and lift requires leverage. Leverage is born from scalable structure. Decide today that sustainability without scalability is a ceiling, not a success. Start measuring your work by how well it multiplies.

Picture a farmer carrying water by hand to every plant in a massive field. He works all day, sweats honestly, and still falls behind the need. Now picture that same farmer installing irrigation lines that water rows at once. Same field, different method, multiplied impact. I once met a consultant who answered every request manually and proudly. He felt valuable but stayed overloaded and capped. When he built templates, training, and packaged solutions, his income grew while his hours stabilized. He did not become less helpful — he became more leveraged. The bucket was replaced by the pipeline. Stop hauling what you could be channeling. Build irrigation for your effort.

Here is the uncomfortable truth that frees future millionaires. Custom-every-time work feels superior but often blocks scale. You say you're being excellent when you're being inefficient. Excellence is not always customization — often it is consistency. A system that delivers reliable value beats a personality that delivers variable brilliance. If your process changes every time, your growth will stall every time. The market trusts repeatable results. Turn your best method into a standard method. Document it, name it, refine it, repeat it. What repeats can expand.

Let me steady you while I stretch you, because this is not about becoming robotic — it is about becoming replicable. You don't lose your humanity when you build systems — you protect your energy. Think of a great teacher who develops a curriculum instead of improvising every lesson. Students learn better and the teacher lasts longer. Structure is not cold — it is compassionate to your future self. You can still personalize within a scalable framework. The framework carries the weight so your creativity can add the spark. Build the frame first. Then decorate it with excellence.

Consider the difference between a live performance and a recorded product. A live show reaches the room. A recorded system reaches the world. Both have value, but only one multiplies without your constant presence. The multimillionaire method asks one powerful question repeatedly. Can this be delivered without me every single time. If the answer is no, redesign it. Record it, automate it, delegate it, or productize it. Free your hours by freeing the process. Time independence is built step by step.

Let's get bold and a little polarizing because this is where many talented people get stuck. Being needed everywhere is not success — it is a scalability failure. If everything breaks when you step away, you built dependency, not durability. Your goal is not to be the hero — it is to be the architect. Heroes get applause and exhaustion. Architects get scale and longevity. Train others, document steps, install checkpoints. Make the work survive your absence. That is not less important — that is more powerful. Replace heroics with frameworks.

Here is a short story that draws a sharp contrast. Two service businesses started with equal demand. One owner did all delivery personally with high touch and high fatigue. The other built a delivery model with training guides and quality controls. The first hit an income ceiling and called it market reality. The second expanded capacity and called it design strategy. Same demand, different destiny. Structure decided scale. Your ceiling is often a system issue, not a market issue. Fix the structure and lift the lid.

Now let's turn this into immediate action you can execute this week. Identify one high-effort task you repeat often. Write every step of how you do it. Simplify the steps until they are teachable. Turn them into a checklist or playbook. Test it by having someone else follow it. Improve the weak spots and retest. Then make that checklist the standard way. You just converted effort into an asset. Repeat this process monthly. Build your library of scalable operations.

You must also scale your measurement or growth will blur. Install dashboards for output, conversion, delivery time, and quality. Numbers reveal bottlenecks faster than feelings. Review them weekly with honesty and speed. Ask what step limits volume. Ask what step limits quality. Upgrade that step first. Small constraint removal creates large capacity gain. Continuous improvement beats dramatic overhaul. Measure to multiply.

Let me speak to your identity now because scalable builders think differently about their role. You are not just a doer — you are a designer of repeatable value. You are not just earning — you are engineering. Say that until your decisions reflect it. Each documented process is a brick in your scalable foundation. Each delegation is a beam in your expansion structure. Each automation is a lever that lifts your load. Build with multiplication in mind. Design for reach, not just relief.

Here is your closing charge and your next move. Take one offer, one process, one workflow and redesign it for scale. Ask how it can reach ten times more people with the same core effort. Remove unnecessary variation. Add necessary structure. Document the path and deploy the system. Test, refine, relaunch. Do not wait for perfect — build for repeatable. If it doesn't scale, it doesn't stay. Choose scale on purpose starting today.

9

EXCUSES ARE EXPENSIVE — OWNERSHIP IS PROFITABLE

Excuses are expensive — ownership is profitable, and whether you like that sentence or resist it will determine how fast you grow. Excuses feel protective in the moment but destructive over time. They comfort your ego while they empty your earning potential. Ownership feels heavy at first but powerful forever. When you take ownership, you take control of the steering wheel instead of criticizing the road. You stop waiting for conditions and start adjusting decisions. The multimillionaire method begins with radical personal responsibility. Not partial, not selective, not convenient — total. You are not a victim of your workflow — you are the designer of it. Say it plainly: if it's not working, I will work it better.

Let me give you a picture that brings this truth into sharp focus. Imagine two drivers stuck in traffic. One spends the whole time complaining about the jam, the weather, the city, and the system. The other looks for exits, alternate routes, and timing patterns. Same traffic, different response, different arrival time. I once coached two founders hit by the same market shift. One blamed the economy for a year. The other rebuilt the offer in a month. Guess who recovered revenue faster. Ownership turns obstacles into instructions. Complaints turn obstacles into anchors.

Here is the hard truth that unlocks forward motion. Every excuse you protect becomes a cost you pay repeatedly. "I don't have time" usually means "I haven't set priority." "I don't have resources" often means "I haven't built resourcefulness." "I'm waiting for clarity" often means "I'm avoiding commitment." These are not character flaws — they are correction points. Excuses feel like explanations but act like brakes. Ownership feels like pressure but acts like power. When you own the outcome, you unlock the options. Replace every excuse with one ownership question: what can I do next. Ask it fast and answer it with action.

Let me steady your heart while I strengthen your spine, because ownership is not self-blame — it is self-leadership. You are not required to control everything, only your response to anything. Think of ownership like grabbing the handles of a heavy machine. The weight is real, but so is the leverage. The moment you say "this is mine to improve," your creativity wakes up. Solutions appear when excuses disappear. Energy returns when blame exits. Progress begins when responsibility enters. This is not harsh — this is liberating. Step into leadership over your own results today.

Consider the small shop owner who says, "Sales are slow," versus the one who says, "My conversion process needs improvement." One states a condition and stays stuck. The other defines a lever and starts pulling. Language reveals ownership level. Owners talk in levers, not labels. They ask what to adjust, not who to accuse. They measure process, not just outcomes. They test messages, not just moods. You must learn to speak in adjustments. Turn every problem into a process question. Then go fix the process.

Let's get bold and a little uncomfortable because comfort with excuses is financial quicksand. Some people can explain their lack of results with stunning detail. They have charts, stories, villains, and timelines. What they don't have is ownership. Detailed excuses are still expensive excuses. The market does not pay for reasons — it pays for results. You can be understood and still be unprofitable. You can be sympathized with and still be stuck. Trade explanation for execution. Results silence what excuses never will.

Here is a story that draws the line clearly. Two team leaders missed the same quarterly target. One blamed the team, the tools, and the timing. The other said, "I failed to build the right system." One kept his pride and lost his progress. The other rebuilt the structure and gained momentum. Ownership accelerated one and froze the other. The difference was not intelligence — it was accountability. Leaders absorb responsibility before they assign correction. Do the same in your business. Take the first share of responsibility every time.

Now let's convert this into immediate profitable behavior. When something goes wrong, write a quick ownership audit. What did I assume that proved false. What did I fail to measure. What did I delay that mattered. What system was missing. What step was weak. Then write one corrective action per answer. Execute those corrections within forty-eight hours. Speed of ownership multiplies speed of recovery. Fast correction beats slow perfection. Make ownership a timed response, not a philosophical idea.

You must also build an ownership ritual so it becomes habit, not heroics. End each workday with a five-minute responsibility review. List three outcomes and your contribution to each. No drama, just data. If you helped it, note it. If you hurt it, own it. If you ignored it, admit it. Then write tomorrow's improvement move beside each one. This ritual turns responsibility into routine. Routine turns growth into momentum. Momentum turns effort into income.

Let me speak to your identity now because profitable ownership is personal before it is procedural. You are not an excuse maker — you are a result builder. You are not here to defend your past — you are here to design your future. Say that until it sounds like you. Then act like it when pressure appears. Identity is forged in moments of responsibility. Each time you own instead of deflect, you level up. Each time you correct instead of complain, you compound progress. Become known to yourself as someone who steps forward, not sideways. That reputation will pay you.

Here is your closing charge and your next step, clear and immediate. Kill one favorite excuse today and replace it with one ownership action. Don't announce it — demonstrate it. Fix one process, make one hard call, launch one delayed move. Do it before your emotions renegotiate your standards. Ownership is profitable because it restores control. Control creates correction. Correction creates results. Results create revenue. Excuses are expensive — ownership is profitable. Choose profit in your behavior starting now.

10

YOU DON'T NEED MORE TIME — YOU NEED FEWER DISTRACTIONS

You don't need more time — you need fewer distractions, and that truth alone can double your output if you dare to apply it. Time is not your tightest constraint — attention is. Everyone gets the same twenty-four hours, but not everyone protects their focus. You say you're overwhelmed, but most days you're over-interrupted. You say you're behind, but you're actually divided. Wealth is built by concentrated effort, not scattered motion. Multimillionaire momentum comes from protected focus blocks, not extended busy hours. The problem is not the clock — it's the clutter. Clear the clutter and the clock becomes enough. Start treating attention like capital instead of background noise.

Picture a magnifying glass under the sun and lock this image into your working memory. Diffused sunlight warms, but concentrated sunlight burns. Same sun, different focus, different result. I once worked with an operator who claimed he needed longer days to grow. We didn't add hours — we removed interruptions. Notifications off, message windows closed, production blocks guarded. His output doubled in ten days without a single extra minute added. Power was never missing — focus was. Concentration converts effort into force. Narrow your beam starting today.

Here is the uncomfortable truth that breaks the distraction habit. Most distractions are not interruptions — they are invitations you accept. The phone buzzes and you bow. The tab opens and you wander. The message appears and you detour. But every accepted distraction is a silent withdrawal from your wealth account. Attention is currency and you are spending it on noise. You don't need better apps — you need stronger boundaries. Distraction is not harmless — it is expensive. Install friction between you and your biggest distractors. Make focus easier than escape.

Let me encourage you while I challenge you, because focus is not a personality trait — it is a trainable skill. You are not broken because you drift — you are unguarded. Think of your mind like a worksite that needs a fence. Without a fence, everything wanders in and nothing gets finished. With a fence, progress compounds. You can build that fence with simple rules. Single-task during value work. Batch communication after production work. Silence alerts during creation work. This is not extreme — this is elite. Build your fence today.

Consider the difference between a deep work hour and a distracted work day. One hour of uninterrupted production often beats eight hours of fractured attention. A writer with no notifications produces chapters. A writer with constant pings produces fragments. A builder who checks tools builds faster than one who checks messages. The wealthy respect cognitive momentum. They enter it deliberately and protect it aggressively. You must learn to stay in the task long enough for depth to appear. Depth is where high-value output lives. Schedule depth, don't just hope for it.

Let's get bold and a little polarizing because this is where results separate. Constant availability is not professionalism — it is productivity leakage. You are not required to respond instantly to everything. You are required to produce meaningfully on something. Instant replies feel useful but often replace important work. Urgent is loud, but important is profitable. Stop letting the loudest item lead your day. Let the highest-value item lead instead. Delay low-value responses without guilt. Advance high-value creation with intensity.

Here is a simple story that lands the point cleanly. Two founders started each morning at the same time. One opened messages first and reacted all day. The other opened projects first and responded later. One felt busy and stayed behind. The other felt focused and pulled ahead. Reaction mode kept one tired. Creation mode made the other wealthy. Same hours, different order, different outcome. Order of attention decides direction of income. Start with creation tomorrow morning.

Now let's turn this into a practical operating system you can apply immediately. Create two daily distraction-free production blocks. Label them and defend them like client meetings. Put your most valuable tasks inside them only. Remove phone, close tabs, mute alerts, and set a visible timer. Work one task until the timer ends. Track completed outputs, not minutes spent. Reward finished deliverables, not prolonged effort. Train your brain to associate silence with production. Repeat this ritual daily.

You must also reduce environmental distraction or willpower will keep losing the fight. Clean your workspace until only priority tools remain. Pre-decide your task list before the block begins. Use website blockers if needed. Put friction on entertainment and speed on execution tools.

Design beats desire every time. Make distraction inconvenient and focus convenient. Small barriers save big hours. Engineer your environment for attention.

Let me speak to your identity now because focused builders see themselves differently. You are not easily pulled — you are deliberately directed. You are not always available — you are intentionally effective. Say that until it shapes your choices. Each protected focus block is a vote for your future wealth. Each ignored distraction is a deposit into your momentum. Identity grows where attention goes. Send your attention where your future lives. Become known to yourself as someone who finishes deep work. That reputation will compound.

Here is your closing charge and your immediate move. Cut three recurring distractions today without negotiation. Replace them with one protected production block. Do it before your habits vote against you again. You don't need more time — you need fewer distractions. Focus is the multiplier you've been missing. Guard it like capital. Use it like leverage. Direct it like a weapon. Your next level of income is hiding behind uninterrupted effort. Go claim it now.

11

TALENT IS OVERRATED — RELENTLESS OPERATORS WIN

Talent is overrated — relentless operators win, and that truth should both unsettle your excuses and energize your future. Raw talent is admired early but discipline is rewarded long. The marketplace does not pay for giftedness — it pays for delivered value. You can be naturally brilliant and consistently broke if you lack operational follow-through. Meanwhile, steady operators with average talent build extraordinary outcomes through repetition. Talent starts races, but operators finish them. Talent attracts attention, but operators collect assets. The multimillionaire method is not built on gifted moments but on governed motion. You don't need to be the most talented — you need to be the most consistent executor. Decide today that consistency will outrank cleverness in your life.

Let me give you a picture that locks this into reality. A high-performance sports car without a driver goes nowhere fast. A reliable truck with a committed driver crosses the country. I once knew two creators in the same industry — one dazzling, one disciplined. The dazzling one impressed rooms and missed deadlines. The disciplined one kept schedules and kept clients. Five years later one had applause and instability. The other had systems and income. Flash attracted praise, but follow-through built profit. Be the driver, not the display.

Here is the uncomfortable truth that levels the field for your benefit. Talent often creates early praise and late laziness. When things come easy, preparation feels optional. When preparation feels optional, consistency collapses. But operators build preparation into routine. They don't rely on natural lift — they install structural lift. They rehearse, refine, repeat, and record. They make their process stronger than their mood. You cannot control your talent ceiling, but you can control your operating floor. Raise your floor and your results rise with it.

Let me encourage you while I press you forward, because this is good news for builders. You don't need rare gifts to build rare results. You need repeatable behaviors applied without drama. Think of a water wheel turning slowly but constantly. It does not rush, but it produces power. Operators think in turns, not bursts. They ask, what can I complete today that moves the machine. They measure finished units, not emotional energy. You are capable of operational excellence starting now. Install your wheel and start turning it daily.

Consider the difference between a sprinter and a marathon builder in business. Sprinters explode with effort and disappear with fatigue. Marathon builders pace with structure and finish with strength. The wealthy are rarely the most explosive performers. They are the most durable executors. They show up when it's boring. They execute when it's repetitive. They improve when it's invisible. Durability beats intensity over time. Train for durability in your habits.

Let's get bold and a little polarizing because this myth needs breaking. Being "gifted" is often used as an excuse for being undisciplined. Some talented people expect outcomes without operations. They want premium results with casual routines. That math never works. Operators respect process more than potential. They build checklists instead of relying on memory. They track metrics instead of trusting instinct. They close loops instead of chasing sparks. Replace gifted identity with governed identity. Become known for reliability.

Here is a short story that draws the line sharply. Two technicians started the same year with equal certification. One relied on natural skill and improvised daily. The other built step-by-step operating procedures. The improviser solved problems but created inconsistency. The operator created consistency and built a team. One stayed solo and stretched thin. The other scaled and strengthened. Skill solved moments — systems solved markets. Choose system-first behavior.

Now let's translate this into immediate action that produces traction. Define your core daily operating sequence tied to revenue and value. Write it in order and follow it without negotiation. Measure outputs at each step. Improve one step per week. Remove guesswork and install sequence. Sequence reduces stress and raises speed. Speed with accuracy builds confidence. Confidence builds capacity. Capacity builds income. Start your sequence tomorrow morning.

You must also build a resilience rule because operators win through pressure, not comfort. When you feel off, you execute anyway at minimum standard. When you feel strong, you execute above standard. Mood adjusts effort — it never cancels effort. Install a "no zero production day" rule. Even small outputs keep the machine warm. Warm machines restart faster. Restart speed protects momentum. Momentum protects morale. Morale protects mission. Keep producing through feeling shifts.

Let me speak to your identity now because operational excellence is personal before it is procedural. You are not a maybe performer — you are a daily operator. You are not waiting for your best day — you are building every day. Say that until it changes your posture. Each completed sequence is a vote for that identity. Each tracked output is proof of your seriousness. Identity grows through evidence, not intention. Collect operational evidence daily. Become predictable in execution.

Here is your closing charge and your next move, clear and immediate. Stop asking where your talent ranks and start strengthening how you operate. Build your checklist, protect your sequence, track your outputs. Execute before you evaluate your feelings. Relentless operators win because they remove negotiation from execution. They show up structured. They deliver repeatedly. They improve continuously. Talent is overrated — relentless operators win. Become one starting today.

12

WEALTH IS BUILT BY DECIDERS — NOT HESITATORS

Wealth is built by deciders — not hesitators, and that line should hit you like a starting gun, not a suggestion. Progress does not belong to the most informed — it belongs to the most committed. You don't get paid for considering — you get paid for committing. Hesitation feels safe because it delays risk, but it also delays reward. Every major income leap begins with a clear, courageous decision. Indecision is expensive because it compounds delay. Decision is profitable because it compresses time. The multimillionaire method is powered by decisive movement, not endless evaluation. You cannot steer a parked car, and you cannot scale a postponed plan. Decide faster and refine in motion.

Let me give you a picture you can carry into every opportunity. Two people stand at the edge of a cold lake at sunrise. One debates the temperature, the wind, the depth, and the timing. The other counts down and steps in. Guess who adapts faster to the water. I once coached two partners reviewing the same deal. One requested six more rounds of analysis. The other made a measured decision and moved. The mover learned through action while the analyzer learned through delay. Speed did not create recklessness — it created feedback. Feedback created advantage. Step in sooner.

Here is the uncomfortable truth that separates builders from watchers. Indecision is not caution — it is often fear wearing a lab coat. It sounds intelligent but behaves avoidant. You tell yourself you are being thorough when you are being protective. But protection can become paralysis. Perfect certainty never arrives before first action. Clarity is usually earned after commitment, not before it. The path lights up when you step, not when you stare. Replace "What if it goes wrong?" with "What will I learn if I go?" Then move.

Let me encourage you while I challenge you, because decisive people are not born — they are trained. Decision is a muscle strengthened by use. Start with smaller choices made quickly and cleanly. Choose the task, choose the method, choose the deadline. Reduce options to increase action. Think of a pilot choosing a runway — once selected, throttle follows. You don't taxi forever — you take off. Your future does not need perfect choices — it needs committed ones. Train yourself to close loops faster. Practice decisive behavior daily.

. . .

Consider the difference between a door that is pushed open and one that is studied for years. One creates passage. The other creates theory. The wealthy push doors and adjust inside the room. They don't demand full blueprints before entry. They enter, observe, and optimize. Movement reveals information that maps never show. You must become comfortable making informed decisions without total certainty. That is not careless — that is operational courage. Courage shortens the distance between idea and income. Push the door this week.

Let's get bold and a little polarizing because hesitation has been overpraised as wisdom. Some people are proud of being "careful" while their opportunities expire. Slow decisions often mean fast regrets. Windows close while committees debate. Markets move while planners polish. Your advantage is not perfect timing — it is timely commitment. Decide within defined limits and move with discipline. Install decision deadlines for key moves. No deadline means no decision. No decision means no momentum.

Here is a short story that draws the line sharply. Two investors saw the same undervalued asset. One waited for perfect signals. The other made a calculated decision with risk controls. The asset doubled before the signals aligned. One protected comfort and lost upside. The other managed risk and gained equity. Same data, different decision speed, different outcome. Risk managed beats risk avoided. You cannot eliminate uncertainty — you can structure it. Decide with guardrails, not guarantees.

. . .

Now let's translate this into immediate action that pays dividends. Create a decision framework for recurring choices. Define your criteria in advance. Set a time limit for evaluation. Choose once criteria are met. Execute immediately after deciding. Review results and refine the framework. This removes emotional drag and increases operational speed. Speed plus structure multiplies progress. Progress multiplies profit. Install your framework today.

You must also build a recovery rule for imperfect decisions because mistakes are teachers, not tombstones. When a decision underperforms, you don't freeze — you adjust. Debrief fast and correct forward. The only fatal error is permanent hesitation. Deciders fail small and learn fast. Hesitators fail slow and learn late. Install a 72-hour adjustment rule after any poor outcome. Analyze, amend, advance. Keep momentum alive.

Let me speak to your identity now because decisive builders see themselves differently. You are not a perpetual considerer — you are a committed mover. You are not waiting for certainty — you are creating clarity through action. Say that until it becomes instinct. Each clean decision is a vote for your future authority. Each closed loop builds self-trust. Self-trust accelerates courage. Courage accelerates opportunity. Become known to yourself as decisive under pressure.

Here is your closing charge and your next move, clear and immediate. Make one delayed decision today and execute the first step within the hour. Stop rehearsing and start committing. Decision is the doorway to momentum. Momentum is the pathway to wealth. Wealth is built by deciders — not hesitators. Choose your direction and move your feet. Refine on the road, not on the couch. Your next level is waiting on the other side of a decision. Step through now.

AFTERWORD

You are closer than you think, stronger than you feel, and more capable than your past results suggest. The distance between where you stand and where you're called to build is not measured in years — it is measured in decisions, discipline, and daily execution. This is the moment where hesitation retires and ownership takes command. You didn't read this far to stay the same. You didn't study these principles to admire them — you came to apply them. Wealth is not reserved for the lucky, the loud, or the naturally gifted. It is built by the committed, the structured, and the relentless. Ordinary days, governed well, create extraordinary outcomes.

Let this be your line in the sand. No more romanticizing potential while tolerating delay. No more collecting ideas without constructing systems. No more blaming limits while ignoring leverage. You now know what moves the needle — decisive action, repeatable process, protected focus, disciplined execution. That knowledge creates responsibility. Responsibility creates power. Power creates movement.

Movement creates momentum. And momentum, sustained long enough, creates wealth.

There will be days when progress feels slow and resistance feels loud. Expect them and move anyway. The builder builds in heat and in cold. The operator operates when it's exciting and when it's ordinary. The decider decides when applause is present and when it is absent. You are not waiting for perfect conditions — you are creating powerful ones. Every finished task is a brick. Every disciplined day is a beam. Every kept promise to your schedule is steel in the structure of your future.

Stand up internally and commit externally. Choose your standards. Run your systems. Guard your focus. Ship your value. Own your outcomes. Adjust fast. Continue forward.

This is not the end of your reading — this is the beginning of your building. Act now. Stay in motion. Finish strong.

ALSO BY DESHAWN PRICE

Toxic Amnesia: When Survival Becomes Self-Destruction

Toxic Strength: When Survival Looks Strong but Feels Empty

Toxic Control: When Fear Disguises Itself as Safety

Toxic Validation: When Approval Replaces Identity

Toxic Loyalty: When Faithfulness Becomes Self-Betrayal

Toxic Forgiveness -: When Grace Is Given Without Boundaries

Toxic Hope: When Waiting Turns Into Wasting Away

The Monetized Viral Machine: How to Build Posts That Pay

The Story-Selling Blueprint: Influence Hearts, Not Just Feeds

Victory Protocol: Strategic Habits That Produce Daily Wins

Your First Million: The Practical Path from Broke to Breakthrough

Millionaire Starting Now — The Fast Track to Seven Figures

The First Million Blueprint — Build Wealth with Precision

www.ingramcontent.com/pod-product-compliance
Lightning Source LLC
LaVergne TN
LVHW090431210926
848480LV00002B/776